WHAT WOMEN SHOULD KNOW ABOUT MEN

By Erica Mary Loberg

CHIPMUNKA CLASSICS

CHIPMUNKA CLASSICS

Published by
Chipmunka Classics
United Kingdom

http://www.chipmunkaclassics.co.uk

Copyright © Erica mary Loberg 2017

ISBN   978-1-78382-342-0

Supported using public funding by

ARTS COUNCIL ENGLAND

LOTTERY FUNDED

Writing is a conversation with yourself
-eml

THAT DRESS

Will you wear that dress?
I asked her
And she doesn't know what I'm talking about

She doesn't know the dress
Rules my nightmares
It sinks inside my balls
It makes me tired
Cause I want to
Have her
In that dress

But I don't have her

To wear it.

VIDEO GAMES

He sits and plays video games
And I wonder

Why do I sit here?

And ponder
On the computer page
I try to make way
By just being
Cool.

While writing.

Or am I just a loser
Like college
Hanging out with a guy
While he plays
Video games

And I don't.

WHAT MUSIC TO PLAY THE NEXT MORNING

What music to play
The next morning
Why is it that you can sleep with someone
And have them inside you
Yet the next morning
With bright naked bodies
Is it so hard.

Do you look at each other in
Your mascara smeared eyes
Or his tired soul?

No.
You don't do that
You put your pretend face on
Cause neither of you can see each other in that eye.

But when you can
After that hot exasperated night
It's still a catch of the eye
Here and there.

So I took a deep breath
And opened up my
Mac book pro
And exhaled a song
Still holding my breath.

VOICELESS

And I am left
Voiceless
By choice
Cause
I don't want to hear the word
Friend
I don't want to hear the truth
I don't want to admit that it's over
So I sit in denial
In reluctancey

Of the truth.

IT SUCKS

I'm a woman
And it sucks

How we think
All the time

What he's doing
What he's thinking
What he wants…

And you never
Even try
To have me
Cross

Your mind.

I DON'T RECALL WAKING UP

I don't recall waking up to
Tears on my bed

Eyes swollen
Almost shut
Red
Tired
Sad

I don't remember
Waking up

Alone
Not just without you

But never with you

Again

FIXATED ON A FIXATION

You never think you are going to be that kind of
woman
The one that riffles through his phone once
Then twice
Then ten+ times

It takes one sex text
From some other woman
To become fixated

Then comes a text from another woman
Then another
Or a reply from him
To that woman
Or the other

Then soon it becomes a terrible

Fixation

Wherever it goes
Your eyes go
Like a child you can take out of your site
Then you become

Fixated on a fixation.

SEPERATED

I didn't want the kitchen table
But I didn't want it thrown at my face

I didn't want the toothpaste
But I wanted my toothbrush

I didn't want to smell your shirt
But I did

I didn't want any of this
Any pain
Any hardship
Anything that would hurt you

But I did.

WHEN WE SHOWER

She puts her head
Beneath the water
When we shower

Together

I watch her hair swing wet
Across her shoulders
And my heart stops
And listens

"Here, it's your turn."

And just like that
We switch places
As she steps outside the shower
I stop and wonder if she knew

You are a glorious beauty!

If only you could hear my heart
Pound in suffocation
As I chock beneath the stream

Of water

That bled throughout your hair
Down your sexy back
Crushing softly on the floor

Now alone I stop and wonder
What she sees
In me

When we shower.

SURFBOARD

I heard her walk into my place
When I was screwing someone else
I ran out looking hard
Flat out

Like a surfboard.

HALF WEEGIES IN THE MORNING

I walked across the room
With my left cheek underwear up my ass
And thought for a never brief second
I should pull it out
I didn't.

WHAT ARE YOU THINKING ABOUT

Sometimes in the early morning
I see him
Staring up in space
Beside me

In bed.

I wonder what he's thinking
Is he worried?
Is he scared?
I can't read his face
To peel apart his mind

And I don't want to be one of those girls that asks…

What are you thinking about?

ONE NIGHT STAND

She's still here
And I'm pissed

I have stuff to do
I want you out of my place
I'm not trying to be rude

But, when you sit in my bed
And don't move
Are you pretending to be asleep?
Do you think your lingering is going to make me
Want you

To stay?

Cause the sun has risen
And I get worried

We had sex last night
Once

And it's time for you to
Go.

AND NEVER COME BACK

"Hey."
It's her.

"What?"
I reply.

"Is now a bad time?"
She asks.

"No, what's up?"
I say.

"Just wanted to check in."

It was my ex-girlfriend.

I came over
We had sex
We ate some blueberries
We had sex again
And now I'm stuck here.

"I have to walk by dog. But I'll be back."

I leave

And never come back.

IN THE MIDDLE OF THE NIGHT

Sometimes I hear her get up
In the middle of the night

She goes to the kitchen
She opens the fridge

And eats.

I don't know why she does that
And I'm afraid to ask her why

Do you have some strange eating disorder?
Why are you eating food?

In the middle of the night.

WET DREAM

Sleep
Never complete
A wet dream
Never felt
Always inside
The ongoing
Mind
Without meaning
Looking for meaning
Sounds so stupid
And wanna
Be
Me.

OUT OF HABIT

Where does that leave us?
You still call me your girlfriend
And I don't ask you
Why do you still call me your girlfriend?
"Out of habit."
He says.
Shit. It hurts.
And you think cause he means it
Or somehow it means, it means
It's not over
Cause it's

"Out of habit."

And you stop kissing me
On the mouth at your greet
And I get a kiss on the cheek
Not that you were ever were a tongue kisser but
Still.
That non-kiss says it all.
You can call me your girlfriend out of "Habit"
But you can kiss my ass
If you're going to say that.
Use that cushion
That I don't sit on
Or an idea
I don't lean on
Yet you use it

Out of habit.

WOMEN'S NIPS

I love your nipples
They're hard
Not soft and sweet
But mean and begging

They want my lips
My tongue
My hardness
To rough up the
Pink

The tower
Of love.

THE KNOCK

Knock
Knock
Knock knock knock.

It's the knock of the

Booty call.

In the middle
Of the night.

You recognize the sound
It knocks you up
The knock knock knock

You want to swallow me now.

I DON'T UNDERSTAND WHY YOUR EMAIL BOUNCED BACK TO ME

I don't understand why your email bounced back to a
me
Closed off back end
No more.

Did you stop your exchange of the other?
Because some woman
Made it crazy
And you had to go into a witness protection program
Which is changing our email
These days?

OR DO YOU JUST WANT TO BE ERASED

EARASED FROM KNOWING ME
KNOWING ANYONE
OTHER THAN THAT SELF
THAT PRETENDS TO CONTINUALLY
NOT KNOW ME.

BUT DO YOU REALLY

KNOW!

SWEATING OUT THE UGLY

I run on the treadmill
After pumping weights
Across my chest

And look around
To the fruitful store
Of women
Sweating out their
Ugly.

AND ELSE AND ELSE AND ELSE

She's my best friend
And were sleeping together as
Friends
But I'm still sleeping with someone else
And else
      And else
            And else.

"I'm not into sleeping with multiple people."
She told me.

"But I love you."

I said it.

I said it after having sex with other women
All over my dick
And now I have one that I want

And she says no

Cause I have sex
A lot
With other women

Along the way.

PUBRITY PART II

I wake up and I'm
Hard

It's like I'm going through puberty
All over again

With you lying next to me

But this time I'm a man
And you're a woman

So I don't need my hand

Just you.

BLIND DATE

It's not exactly a blind date but
I wasn't exactly sober
When I met him

Did I tell him what I do?
Did I talk about Downtown?
Can I wear heels?

It's not a blind date
But

I'm not quite sure what he looks like.

MESSY

I told her I love you
I didn't think it through
It just came out.

Then she pulled away
From my arms.

Cause she knew I was a mess
Messing around with other
Women.

I thought
"But I love you"
Would fix
The mess
I've made.

But it didn't.

It only made things more

Messy.

ALL THE TIME

Shit
Shit
She's texting me like a
Crazy person

After seven texts I have to
Reply

"Hey, what's up?"
And a quick response back
"Hi!! What are you up to?"

I didn't mean to wait to reply
But I did

"I'm busy."

Like that means anything to you
Cause you expect my response

Quick like yours

All the time.

SHE DID IT IN MY SHEETS

She did what?
He asked his friend.

She did it
In the sheets
That she borrowed
In the room
That she's renting
In my apartment
Ok
I don't know if I should be happy for her
Or scared
I'm in an alter state of disbelief
Not because she's a virgin
But because she did it
In my sheets
Which is fine!
I guess
I don't know.

ON THE TIP OF MY TONGUE

My girlfriend has her period
But I don't keep track of it
And when it comes around

Fragile words
Sit on
The tip
Of my tongue

They sit there waiting
And tempt my carnal urge
To ask

You wanna try…

SHE CUT OFF HER HAIR!!

I should have said
Something
When she asked
About losing her luscious locks
Of hair

But I didn't.

"You're pretty no matter what."

Then she walked through the door
She seemed to be
So free
So happy.

And looked for me to say
"Oh my God no wayyyy
I absolutely love it!"

NOOOOO.

WHY AREN'T WE MARRIED?!

"We are practically married!"
He says

"But we're not."
She says

And it has been over
Toooooo many years

Living
Here together.

Does he think that means
We're married?

I think that means we're not.

And we're probably never going to.

LEGS

I don't know how guys sit
With their legs spread open
Left to right
Magnifying their Id
And I have to cross mine.

FAKING IT

I'm tired of faking it
And I wonder if he knows

I've been doing it for
Ages

Forever shall
Be told

I have it down
Like a hammer

While I'm being
Nailed

The Oscar goes
To me!

Is this my betrayal?

LOSING YOU

So I have been in therapy
For over a year
Cause you asked me to.

And although I know my tendencies
I can't seem to
Conquer them.

I still walk hard
I still eat the same food
I love you so much
That sometimes I wish it was

Before you had a man.

Cause before you had a man
You were on my phone
You were in my back pocket

My savior.

I took it for granite
That you'd be there
All the time
At any time
For
Me

WHY I DON'T LET GUYS BUY ME A DRINK

He asked me if he could buy me a drink
I don't know the last time someone asked me that

I usually buy the guy
A drink

So I'm not one of those girls that
Let's guys just buy them drinks
For free

It sounded refreshing
I could try
Not being
The hard core girl
Maintaining control
With my own wallet
Funding my liberty

So I said yes.

After

He asked me for my number
I didn't want to
But I gave it out

Why?

Cause I felt guilty?
Cause he bought me a drink?
And I said ok?

This is why I don't let guys buy me a drink.

LOSS

I never found anyone to replace you
So I worked hard
To
Replace
Me

It took
Minutes, hours, days, weeks, months, years

Therapy
Psychiatry
Pills
Booze
Running
Reading
Writing
Thinking

Denial
Defeat
Defense

To find myself

Again

And I'm not sure I found me
And know I didn't replace me

Or lose you.

HE CAME INSIDE ME

It trickles out of you
Soft and slow
After a condom breaks
In the midmorning
Down the sides
Of your insides
Soft and sure
Untamable
Undetermined
Just sailing low
Like the water that runs down your dashboard window
In a Sunday carwash.
It slides from the top
To the ground
Smiling all the way…

HOUSEWIVES

Housewives here
Housewives there

All she does is watch
Housewives

New York
Atlanta
Beverly Hills…

All and all she gets her thrills

How many Housewives will you see
Before you come to bed

With me.

NOT

I asked you one time if I was good in bed
I knew that I was
I just wanted to hear it from your voice

"Are you kidding? You're fantastic!!"

Glad I left you
Glad I moved on
You fuck like shit
My hand was always better bitch

It's nice to wake up to texts
From an EX
After six months of being apart
Sure sounds like you moved on

Thanks for letting me know
You sure have

NOT

DO YOU HIDE YOUR WALK OF SHAME?

Do you hide your walk of shame?
Cause I don't

When I wake up
Next to
I don't know
And break lose
Out onto the street

It's early morning
People are coffee
Put together
Walking normal

And I carry myself
Home
With mascara running down my back
A lost earring on the side of my face
A painful walk
In my heels

Thank God I have a jacket
To cover the mess
Beneath the coat
Of
Wrinkled clothes
And underwear stuffed
In my pocket
Hair a mop on my head

So I decide to strut

Embrace the walk of shame
Some people call it a walk of fame

What do you call it?

"HOW MANY MEN HAVE YOU SLEPT WITH?"

"How many men have you slept with?"
It was the first session with her psychiatrist.

"Ah…."
She had NO idea.

"Ten, twenty, fifty, a hundred?"

"Ah…"
She didn't know her number.

"Why don't you multiply all those numbers together…
…And then we'll start there."

THE TRUTH HURTS

Blah blah bah so what do you want from me?

My soul
My life

My go to girlness?

What exactly do you want from me?

Other than

Not me.

IT'S LIKE OUR BODIES WERE MADE FOR EACH OTHER

It's like our bodies were made for each other

It was the first time we've been naked together
In bed
After years of friendship

I love your body
He told me

Seven years later
After our relationship
After our breakup
In bed
And I think about the first time
We had sex and he said
It's like our bodies were made for each other

Now I sit here and think of that first time
Then I think did you say that
To all the other girls?
Even when he was with me?

It's like our bodies were made for each other.

WRITING

It's easy to write
When you have experiences

But when you isolate
Don't masturbate
Or get laid

Your mind runs dry
And the pen runs old.

LET ME GO

Is he drunk?
Is he high?
Pounding at my door
When there is no reply?

How many times will you call me
And never get a hello?

How many texts will you send me
Until you let me go.

THE BLACKOUT

I'm so hung over
I want to die

Yet

Somehow I managed to get home
Somehow I managed to fold my clothes
Somehow I managed to get his number

Yet

Somehow I forgot his name
Somehow I end up looking lame
Somehow I look through my phone and wonder

Is this the guy that has my number?

MATCH.COM

Everyone lies on match.com
Right?

I showed up to her place and saw her
Peep through the door

Then close it real fast
Like I didn't see her

I couldn't tell when I entered her place
If she was disappointed

Pictures are hard
Obviously I'm not photogenic but...

Ring ring ring
She took a call
And seemed concerned

I have to go
It's work calling

Oh, ok
So I left

Everyone lies on match.com

A BAD MEMORY

I smell your dick
on my fingertips

i'm not sure if i'm
disgusted
after mistake sex
last night
or happy to have the memory of our time
together

but I don't want to lick it

so I must not like it

it's a bad memory

SPARK

Spark
Spark
Spark

She seemed to take pleasure in my pain
As the thread sparked off my face
Even breaking the string

"You haven't ever threaded before?"

I think my face saved me from an answer

She continued to thread my brows
And I closed my eyes
To stop a hairy tear from
Dropping to the floor
Where I'm sure there was a mess

"Do you need a break?"

I smiled and made a face to keep going

So she did

I never had my eyebrows threaded
I heard about waxing
I knew about plucking

But never thought it was something

Like THIS.

AND I DIDN'T KNOW WHAT TO DO

I wanted to make love to her
But she climbed onto
Me

And I let her
Of course

She ate my shirt
She kissed my toes
She squeezed my flesh
She said to lie down
She took over my whole body

And I didn't know what to do

GAY GUYS LIKE TO DRESS UP GIRLS

He came over with bags of things
Not makeup or anything
But things he was going to try on
And made a stance in front of the mirror
And took two seconds to get himself together
For the night

And now it's my turn

The make-up comes out
Bam bam bam
The brush hits the pallet
And scrubs my face

Open
Open
I open my eyes and my lashes sit scared
As he dives into the colors again
And again
And I have no idea

What's the end?

He rips through my closet
Throwing clothes
On the bed, over the chair
Anywhere
Everywhere

And I try this on
And that on
And finally

I am ready to go

I look in the mirror and ...

Gay guys like to dress up girls.

HIS FINGERS

He brushes the fingers of his hand on my leg
He waits a small pause in between the brush strokes
And you move your leg to your side
Cause it tingles and your now ready
Not sure what that is for him
If anything.

AND SO SHOULD I

I screwed up last night
I did it again
I fucked him
And woke up to a bloody mess
We didn't care that I had my period
So we just did it

And my sheets
Stamp mark every
Thrust and hit
On my insides

The sheets are done
And so should I.

TOGETHERNESS

I sat on the stoop and wrote her my love letter
And held onto it

We were at a club
In London

I told her
When a bus goes by
With a Calvin Klein model
I think it's you

She stayed stiff

At least say something, please
I said with wondering eyes, and a desperate reach for an
answer

And she sipped her drink

And said nothing.

He was my friend
I never thought of him as a lover
And he hit me with a ton of bricks

I'm wearing a target shirt with plain black pants
I'm not a supermodel on a bus

And his eyes wandered into mine
Looking for some truth
What do you think?

We spent the night before staying in a motel with our
friends
Bed by bed
And held hands
Across the space between his mattress and mine

And thought to myself
That hand to hand touch wasn't just that
It was a heavy hand that loved one

To another.

LIPS ON MY NECK

I felt her lips simmer close to my neck

It reminded me of our first time together
She sat on my couch and rested by my head

Then she kissed me

She kissed my neck
And we went to bed

Now

Years later

I feel her lips ready to quake
Right in that hungry spot
The same place on my neck
As before
And I wait for her to kiss me
Again

But she didn't.

CAUSE YOU BROUGHT ME TO THIS

Yeah I will resort to name calling

Bitch

Fucker

Whore

Asshole

I'll resort to all of it, bitch

Cause you brought me to this.

BUT I AM IT

I don't think she knows
How insecure I am

I don't say it
I try not to show it

But I am it

YOU WERE MY SONG

Most people have a song
With their lover
Their friend
Their Ex
Someone

You were my song

I heard it when you laughed
In the car
I saw it when you
Danced
In your apartment

I heard you
In my ear
Every time
You played
With me

You were my song.

BOUNCE

"I'm gonna need you to bounce soon."

Was the text she saw
On her boyfriends phone.

Bounce…?
What does that mean?
Like, I want to play basketball?
No.

It means I want you to
Bounce

On my dick.

ELEVATOR

She stepped into the
Elevator

Her lips surveyed my outside
And I took it in

Then took
Her in

I grabbed her into my arms
And kissed her hard

Maybe she thrashed herself
Onto me
First

I don't recall.

HE DOES NOT GIVE A SHIT

It's not like I slave over his texts
Or anything

I stand in the shower
I run on the treadmill
I sit quietly
I drive my car
I rest in bed

But
There is no resting

When it's all about him.

RISK

It's hard to take risks
I hear it everywhere
But what if your whole life

Is a risk

FEAR

You can't just live in fear
Even though you have to

Cause what else you are going to do

When you have to eat
Buy toilet paper
Feed your dog

How are you suppose to say
No fear

When fear is always going to be

A realistic factor

Of life.

CHARACTER

How do you define a man?

Character
Honesty
Integrity
Loneliness
Love
Hope
Death
Dark
Depth
Soul
Power

How do you define a man?

I think character
Says it

All.

I DIDN'T CALL YOU BACK

I met you
I held your hand
I walked with you
Together

I held you strong
Beat you down
Into my heart
And you breathed into
My mouth

And I didn't call you back.

"YOU KNOW I CAN FEEL EVERYTHING RIGHT?"

She doesn't get it.

I feel her vagina
Sucking in my
Dick
And when she climaxes
It releases itself onto me.

"You know I can feel everything right?"

(no, I didn't)

ON THE TREADMILL

Running deep on the rubber track strip
Breathing hard
And wondering when
You'll stop thinking
Of him
Again
And now
And when

Will it end.

Over and over he runs
Through your head
As you race like
Treading water

On the treadmill.

And try to lose the thought
Of him
As you drown in your sweat

On the treadmill.

TO DO IT

How do you write a break up letter
To someone you love?

I can't seem to open my mouth

I guess I can't do it in person
But I've never written a letter before

I refuse to do it in a text.

So I'll just keep being in the relationship
And hope she
Breaks up with me

How miserable do we have to become
Till one of us
Has the balls

To do it.

IT'S NOT FAIR

I remember when I wrote
Habanera Blowjob
And burnt a dick

Now I want a dick
Something outside of my
Body to yank hard
Pull
Take charge
Own it.

You can't own a
Vagina
Cause it is outside the inside.

It is the most frustrating
Part of the body

Which is not fair.

Women can't yank on
Their dick
They can't even rub it
Hard
To the point of oblivion
They have to
Search
Hunt
Rough it up like sand paper
And even then
It's not enough

It's not fair.

IT'S NOT A SECRET BUT STILL IS

It's not a secret

But we keep it to ourselves

Ours shame
Our embarrassment
A loss of dignity
Of intelligence

Integrity

Are terrible things to question

But I do

When you love someone that betrays you
And you still think of him
Your good times together

You're left with a secret

And you can't stop being there

Inside his world
That wouldn't be yours

But still is.

I DON'T EVEN EAT CHIPS

I don't even eat chips
They just happened to be there

Cause my friend bought them
Like it was normal.

Ah….no...skinny bitches
Don't buy chips.

That was yesterday

And today…

I have chips on my desk
While I listen to
Pink Floyd
And recall when it became a song
For us
Between us

I stood in the kitchen
With a jean shirt and a
Halter-top
With argyle
Embedded in the
Knit.

And this song played "Wish you were here."

And at that time
It meant
Nothing.

Now
It will always mean something before the heartache
The fall out of myself.

Now I can hear it with my new chips
That I never would have bought

Without a friend.

I GOT A TEXT FROM AN OLD FLAME

I got a text from an old flame
Asking me how I'm doing
What's up?

It's exciting to get texts
From women from my past

And they still have me in their phone
And they still call me

For whatever reason
I don't care
But it jumps my heart
It makes me smile

It gives me some
Hope

That I still
Have her.

LETTER

I keep pouring my whiskey
And look through my YouTube options
For music
Guns n Roses
Keeps showing up

So I listen to Estranged
Pass by Rocket Queen
And then there's Axel on the mic
With Patience

I hit it

And recall a love letter I gave a girl I had loved
Or maybe a crush
I don't know

I don't think she ever knew

But, as I sit here now
I feel different
Hearing the song

I feel that feeling I had
Back when I wrote it

I felt sure
At the time
That I loved her

But now....

ON MY SIDE

And I have to breath another side of relief
That I'm not pregnant
Cause you pull out
And think that's
Birth control
When it's not

And then I think about women
That try to get pregnant
And can't
And hold my breath
When I shouldn't even be
In this situation
When it's my situation
That I made and
Continue to make
Every time

Stop putting your naked dick in my face
Stop slowing down the world
To think
It's going to always be

On my side.

THE UNUSED CONDOM

I woke up severely hung over
I called in
Sick

I slept the morning away
Thanking God that sleep
Disappears a foggy night

And I opened the curtains
Above my head
And there it was

An unused condom on the windowsill.

Earlier that morning
When I went through the fridge to guzzle down
coconut water
I saw the wrapper on the floor
Beside the bed

And thought
Good

But now I see the unused condom by my head
On my window sill

And wonder
What the fuck?

4TH OF A HIGH

4th of a high
the party hits July
Walking thru
the maze
in the haze
of weed
home
resting in
the bones.

PAAALEEZE

He got up and ran to the bathroom
To check his dick

He thought it was blood
But his dick was blank

"I don't have my period you know."

"That must be your feminine juices."

He laughs like he's cool and funny.
Like he came up with that on his own.

Juices?
Do you think I'm an idiot?

We've slept together for yearssss
Without a word about anything.

And now you have some catch phrase you try to own
As your own?

Who did you bang that told you that?

PAAALEEZE.

I DON'T GET IT

I don't get it
I don't know why you are still
Crying

We've been over for over a year
And you're still knocking down
My door

We loved each other
We'll love again

Just not here
Not now

HAIR

I died my hair today
I straightened it

It looks amazing.

It takes a lot to keep this up
Every day

It's not like I need to keep it up
To get a guy
But

It helps.

BECAUSE OF YOU

I rip my dick
across the flesh
of my hand
as I try and

masturbate.

thinking of you
thinking of porn
thinking of something

sometimes I have trouble
thinking

cause
my image is broken

because of you.

TINDER

Swipe left
Swipe right
Swipe right
Swipe right
Swipe left
Swipe right

You got a match!

Yes….sweet…finally!

Then I realize that swiping
Right means
Yes I'm into you
And swiping left means
No I'm not

Great.

BUYING
TAMPONS AT CVS

Thank God I got my period
Not that I've been unsafe or anything
It's good to be paranoid though
Nothing's full proof.

Do I grab my regulars?
And I'll be out of here?
But…
I've been having sex with a bigger dick lately
So I'll pick up
Super absorbent.

I'm probably all stretched out
Anyway
Well…..

It's better to be safe
Then sorry.

THE HIGHER ROAD

What's the higher road?

He fucked *me* over
And *I'm* supposed to take
The higher road?

When you're name gets smeared across the flesh of
outsiders?

I step into the elevator
And see one of his friends
Hiding from me
Head down
Discombobulated

Did he tell you
Terrible things
About me
And now you're scared
Dismissive

So what am I supposed to do?

Pretend I don't know
That were stuck in an elevator
With you pretending to not know me
Me pretending that I don't know you're here

And the doors open
For me to exit
And I turn my head to the side
And take a good look
Give a good look
At you

Despite what you've heard
About me
Bad, sad, crazy, depressed.

I'm here
It's me

It's me here now

AND THE FURY CONTINUES

You love someone
Hard
They ..

And the unclarity continues

While you drop dead at the surface
Of honesty

And he walks like coffee is normal in the morning.

And you love him
And you don't know
What he thinks

I JUST FIGURED IT OUT

You don't want to know my insides
I can't do this
What?
You say women don't ever complain
After the bed shells
And you never asked if they
Ever were satisfies

Sensually.

A FRIEND THAT IS NOT JUST FRIENDS

You make a
Mistake
Cause you're lonely
And take advantage
Of an open space
And he sleeps there
Beside you
With you
As your friend
But who knows what it is for him.

Shit.

A friend that wants you
You think
Or just ignore
As happening.

A friend that is not just friends

I SOFTLY

I softly melt the skin
Across your back
With a steep rub
And roll my fingers down your leg
Feeling you slowly breathe to attention
Reaction
Loving the sensation
Of the human touch.

And I roll my fingers
Up and down
Up and down
Your back
Not even smelling your skin
Just collecting dead skin
Beneath my fingernails

And it's with me.

COURAGE KNOWS WHAT NOT TO FEAR -
PLATO

I have loved you
Like no other in
My life.
My existence.
You're my heart.
You're my mind.
You are my tragedy.

You are my pain
You are my need
You are my living love

That I try to forget.

EVEN IF

Even if I don't walk it
Even if I don't say it
Even if I don't know it

I love you.

www.ingramcontent.com/pod-product-compliance
Lightning Source LLC
Chambersburg PA
CBHW032048040426
42449CB00007B/1034